OUT OF SILENCE:

A Personal Transformation

Christine

Happy trails to you

Jm Wsde

OUT OF SILENCE:

A Personal Transformation

ANN WADE

Ivy
House
Publishing Group
www.ivyhousebooks.com

PUBLISHED BY IVY HOUSE PUBLISHING GROUP
5122 Bur Oak Circle, Raleigh, NC 27612
United States of America
919-782-0281
www.ivyhousebooks.com

ISBN: 1-57197-421-0
Library of Congress Control Number: 2004103652

Printed in the United States of America

To all my teachers who were there when the student was ready.

Preface

MY STORY IS written fourteen years after the experience itself. The front end of it really began in the late 1970s when I was seeking ways to relieve a painful, emotional situation. My search led me through numerous books, seminars, and teachers—I absorbed and I pondered. I began the exercise of daily alpha relaxation sessions, and, with the use of new affirmations, my thinking and beliefs changed. My answers were to be found within myself, and so began the letting-go process of looking outside myself for the states of happiness, love, and self-worth. I traveled a new path, began a new spiritual journey, and like a magnet, I could not pull away. My 1988 experience solidified all of those learnings into a new beginning—a crisper path, a deeper spirituality.

I kept a daily journal of that September, which has been a reference for the sequence of and my inner responses to the episodes that unfolded. I have expanded the insights and reflections of my original journal entries as the footprint of time and personal life changes made from 1988 onward has brought deeper understanding to the initial thoughts. I make a distinction between insights and reflections. Insights are those immediate learnings that come in a flash and I accept as Universal truths. Reflections arise from the processing of my thoughts, and these I accept as personal truths.

These truths encountered in 1988 remain true for me today; they are now integrated into my being and daily activities. September 1988 was a fork in the road of my spiritual journey. It was a defining moment in a point of time that reshaped my thinking processes and my patterns of behavior.

Terms used in the spiritual realm have distinct definitions for each individual; therefore, certain words need to be defined for my story.

Self is the part of me that lives in the walking-around, material world where facts and ego are dominant. Here the ego is concerned with the control of mental thoughts and the acquisition of things.

Higher Self is the part of me that lives in the inspirational world where intuition and quick insight prevail, where wisdom and spirit dwell. Higher Self is interchangeable with Spirit and Soul.

Universe is the broadest concept of space, time, and

consciousness. The Universe has a harmonious order—in its principles and systems—processes that have a constant repeatability. Cosmos and Universe are interchangeable.

God is interchangeable with **Divine** and is the original intelligence, the creation of all there is. The fundamental source of Being. The ten thousand things of Tao.

Love is the non-physical love coming from the abundance of kindness, unselfishness, generosity, humility, and cooperation. Love arising for the collective whole versus individual satisfaction.

In writing with the hindsight of fourteen years, I see more distinctly how this one experience transformed my life. My story describes the events as they truly happened and is enriched by meaning and understanding that became more evident with time. The insights realized guide me to this day. I believe these types of experiences are not unique or uncommon; it's just that this experience was uniquely mine.

Acknowledgments

To my sister Jo Wagner, my daughter Valerie Del Curto, and my friend Mary Nelson, who encouraged me to write my story. To the members of my Writer's Group in Iowa City, who listened to my readings and gave valuable feedback and suggestions. They are professional writers and their support meant a lot to me. And, most importantly to my neighbor and most talented friend, Judith Sutherland, who fulfilled the primary role of editing and who with questions and probing helped me to bring clarity to the expression of my story. I am grateful for her time and efforts that she generously gave to my writing. I must add my appreciation for the staff of Ivy House Publishing Group who designed my story into a lovely piece of art. They made this publication a pleasurable experience for me.

Heading North

THE BEGINNING OF this day was not the start of any ordinary day. It was six in the morning, the first of September, 1988, and I was headed north out of Minneapolis on Interstate 35 to an adventure that had been in the making for over five years. The morning light was being held back by a dark sky threatening thunder, downpour, and lightning. Driving into this horrific thunderstorm was not the beginning I would have expected for the peaceful solitude toward which I was heading.

Looking back, maybe the electrifying beginning was meant to catch my attention for the significance of the journey I was embarking upon. This solitary, thirty-day retreat was like fate, a matter of necessity, no choice of "to do or not to do." Its incubation began in 1982 and played out in endless scenarios up to a year ago.

It had begun with a knowing, my intuitive inner voice giving a strong sense that I was destined for a month's retreat in solitude—a private space for me to find my relationship with me, with spirit, with nature, with the cosmos—new learnings to recognize and integrate. That initial thought grew in intensity and perfection over time. The very first inner message was a quick hint, not precise, open to possibilities, and vulnerable to my ego-laden interpretation. Ah, the Pacific Ocean, an island, exotic and sensual. More pleasurable places rose in my mind, like Mazatlan, Bermuda, Santa Fe, Bulgaria, Tahiti, Bora-Bora, and even southern California. However, none of them would ripen to any degree, and I finally let go of my desire for them. It became quite clear that I was exercising one of my typical characteristics: "I shall direct, plan, organize, and make this happen to my satisfaction"; that is, "I shall be in control of this retreat." The longer I persisted in maintaining control, the more dubious each of my desires became.

I came to the realization that I could let go and let my retreat, its purpose and location, come about in natural order. So I did let go and put my trust in a higher power to direct this state of affairs. From then on, "perfect order" was exactly what happened.

Ann Wade

First Insight: *Some Higher Self is in charge and will make known, in the right order and time, all one needs to know. Subtleties, essential and unseen, work beneath the surface. The longer one attempts to control, the more one becomes a barrier to the rightful unfolding of the happening itself.*

The Message

I AM BLESSED with the faculty of receiving messages in words present to the inner ear—internal messages that prove to be trustworthy. I call this my inner voice. One year prior to heading north, I began to hear the particulars of the retreat. It would be one month. It would be September 1988. It would be beside water. It would be travel by car. It would be solitary—no other companion, in person or on TV.

Old mental habits took my thoughts to the many lovely seaside places I had always wanted to visit. I began to envision the surroundings and the house. However, my visions would not fit together—they just would not jell into a definitive picture, and I gave the ideas a rest. Three days later during a morning shower, my internal voice was loud and clear—Grand Marais on Lake

Superior. This was certainly at an opposite pole from the exotic places that I had been thinking of. Grand Marais is on the northern-most tip of Minnesota, sixty-five miles from the border of Canada. I had been there once with a friend several years before for a long weekend and found Grand Marais to be a quaint, small community—busy with vacationers during summer months and settling into a family of locals during winter months.

Following my mental directive, I was soon on the phone to locate a rental property agency in Grand Marais, wondering if one year advance reservation was out of the norm. My contact gave assurances that I was calling just in the nick of time, for they had few rentals left fitting the specifications I set forth: by the shores of Lake Superior, no other cabins or houses within sight or sound, absence of traffic noise, and an outside porch.

Within a week, the agency sent pictures and descriptions of possible rentals and told me to choose as soon as possible. Two cabins met the criteria. One had a most attractive eating area surrounded by windows, overlooking the water. While my desire wanted to make it my choice, I was faithful and relinquished the selection to higher self. When I called the agency, I found my preference had been removed from the rental listing that very morning by the owners. So the choice was made for me, and the second cabin became my nest for September of 1988. Within a week the what, where, and when was decided—sight unseen. As I signed and sent my deposit check, it all felt absolutely right. And now I could indulge in the luxuries of preparing for my journey.

At this point the other unknown, the purpose for the retreat, became known. It was in a morning meditation that I pictured a bright golden path and heard the words "be still and listen." It was to be a time of stillness—a time for reflection and learning the richer design of life and soul. It was to be a time of awareness—a time to accept other undertakings for this lifetime. It was to be a time of forgiveness—of self and others. It was to be a time to set a new course—of letting go of old ways and embracing new ones. By now, my retreat began to take on an enticing and exciting overtone.

Second Insight: *Circumstances connect and merge into a whole smoothly, rapidly, and easily when one accepts and heeds the inner voice. A desire to control interrupts the natural pattern and flow of life events; the Higher Self has more wisdom than the Ego.*

September 1st

3:56 A.M. I AWAKE FROM a deep sleep to a loud clap of thunder, like the gods saying "Get up and on your way." I lie silently in bed for a few moments to let my anticipation have full rein.

5:15 A.M. Pack the last few things into the car, which has no room left. Books, blankets, clothes for both warm and cold weather, golf clubs (for an alternative to hiking), writing books and materials, radio and favorite tapes (for weather reports and music), and food.

6:30 A.M. On the road—dark sky and heavy rains. Road markings are faint to the eye. The heavy 1976 Chevy Impala holds the road.

9:30 A.M. Breakfast in Duluth at my favorite diner, the Lemon Drop. It's not my favorite anymore.

10:30 A.M. Stop at Gooseberry Falls. Walk down the path to stand on the rocks underneath the falls and take in the sparkling beauty. Return through the trees, lush, green, and wet with rain.

12:15 P.M. View Grand Marais across a span of Lake Superior. The town sits out on a point and is dimly outlined. I stop along the bend in the road to take a picture and wonder what is to follow.

12:30 P.M. Arrive at Grand Marais and locate the agency for keys and directions. A mailbox, designed as a red barn, is the landmark for the cabin one mile north of town.

1:00 P.M. The drive from the mailbox to the cabin winds through a canopy of trees and down a sloped drive right onto the green lawn of the cabin. I unlock the door and step into September. The cabin is clean, uncluttered, nestled in a gathering of trees and within hearing of water lapping the shore. With one exception the cabin is exactly as I had envisioned. The kitchen, stretching along the north wall, is much larger than my mental picture. Unpack the car, finding plenty of space along the bedroom wall for all the boxes.

2:30 P.M. Walk the short path to the rocky bank overlooking the lake—the waves are coming in with such a roar. An ideal spot for morning meditation, midday sunning, and evening angelus. The water and the power of the lake will cleanse the spirit and body.

3:00 P.M. Put a lounge chair up on the porch that extends the length of the cabin and read *Cassidy* by Morris West. As the afternoon chills, I wrap up in my old favorite afghan.

6:30 P.M. A light supper at the kitchen table with a full view of the lake. The entire wall along the kitchen and living room is glass with a full-length porch on the other side. My evening prayers give celebration for my nest and the beauties of nature surrounding it. It seems to be perfect order!

7:30 P.M. Snuggle down under several layers of covers. Sleep comes immediately. Awake at 3:20 A.M. to hear rain on the roof. Doze off until 6:15 A.M. I awake to the sound of lapping water and to a morning sun shining through haze over the horizon. And so it begins.

My cabin.

Settling In

I SANK INTO the luxury of doing nothing. I relished the hours without demands. I gave way to reverie and meditation. My eyes filled with the color of fall leaves. My ears sang with the music of the wind and water.

My nose relished the smell of fresh, pure air. The morning sun awakened my spirit and the evening sunset honored my being. I was experiencing an answer to old yearnings for freedom.

I lingered in the cabin and nearby woods for several days. I indulged in ten to twelve hours of sleep a night. My dreams were numerous, vivid, and often sequential. It seemed my subconscious was processing a buildup of many years, and I became intrigued with identifying dream symbols. I idled away hours by the lake and let the sound of the lapping water wash over my being. I gazed at the storms moving across the lake and gasped at the beauty of the rainbows that followed. I ambled along the three-mile road that looped north of the driveway, taking note of each bird, leaf, and insect. I reclined on a lounge, reading in the sunlight. So went my first week.

> ❦ *Reflection:* It's like going off with a lover—to enjoy each other, to become closer, to see through the eyes of love, to be content just to be in the presence of love. No, there's no aloneness here. There's me, Ann, and the only other love there is—in the breeze, on the clouds, with the waves, in the quiet woods—surrounded day and night. Any loneliness was before now and will find no place in time forward.

> ❦ *Reflection:* To snuggle into the warmth of covers after a chilly walk on the porch at three o'clock in the morning is to draw back into a cocoon, both physically and mentally. I know no other place for the physical body and no other space for the mind at this moment. Just this small, tight, warm, dark cocoon, and I seem to melt into a nothingness—awaiting transformation.

I knew stillness and silence was destined when a funny thing happened with the portable radio that I'd brought along for a bit of company. First, I tried a Neil Diamond tape of favorite songs; it played out about eight bars of music and went dead, not to operate again for the entire month. When I searched for a radio station, only an early morning weather announcement tuned in from Michigan each day, and then there'd be no more reception. I laughed and laughed at myself, finally realizing that the higher self was deadly serious about the seclusion of this month.

I began to really know that this thirty-day solitude was more than a respite from daily demands of life. The purpose was more than that, and at last it became clear to me. Here in this silence, I would be a vacuum in which the essence of my relationship with nature and universe could be defined. Here in this silence, voids could be filled with the higher self, and the divine side of creation could be experienced. Here in this silence, I could begin the integration of unconditional love. With those thoughts in mind, I went for a walk along the lake.

❖ *Reflection:* I am a part of nature but behave as if I am not. All other species are nurtured and cared for by the Universe. Humans must come to that knowledge. Nature has a rhythm, and all species live to the ebb and flow of that rhythm. Humans must come to that knowledge. I am amused at my feelings of self-importance; I smile at how hard I work to be indispensable; I laugh at my thoughts that the world can't advance without me. Arrogance walks hand in hand with control, Ann. Why not stand tall in present moment like a tree and trust God to care for you as part of nature?

First Excursions

ON THE SIXTH day, I left my cabin surroundings and took my first hike, toting my backpack containing lunch and water. Ten minutes up the road was Judge C. R. Magney State Park, where I'd find the head of the Kettle Falls trail. The parking lot was empty of cars, so I knew I had the trail pretty much to myself, which seemed appropriate to one who hungered for silence.

The trail ambled amid trees and came out to the top of a bluff overlooking the Brule River. In the distance, the water cascaded down three levels and was copper brown from water draining through mineral-soaked ground. Thus, I saw the significance of the name Kettle Falls.

The trail was a steep staircase down to the river at the bottom. Several lookout points jutted off the trail from where one heard different melodies from the cascading water. I stood in awe as my eyes took in the banks of evergreen trees and the sparkling bubbles of water. I walked beyond the trail at river bottom, finding a small clearing next to the water edge where I became spellbound by the flowing water. Time paused—it was just me and the universe. I lingered until my spirit was overflowing with serenity, until my senses had saturated every nuance, until my body could freely leave.

I ate my peanut butter sandwich and apple, leaving the core under a tree for some forest animal. I knew I'd be back on this trail again before month's end.

I returned by way of the Gunflint Trail road, which winds for a short stretch above Grand Marais and Lake Superior. It was the end of the afternoon, and the sunlight streaked across the lake as I stood on the bluff and sent my gratitude out along the airways. The day, the scenery, the silence affirmed how perfect the selection for my retreat was.

I awoke early the next morning to sit on the front porch watching daybreak. The sky lightened with a horizontal pink band across the lake. The color of the band turned from pink to a bright rose and then to orange/red when the sun appeared as a small red dot on the horizon. The sky had not even a wisp of a cloud, and the orange reflections on the water were radiant ripples of gold. Ah, and the silence too was golden.

After this majestic scene, I turned to the mundane, exploring Grand Marais and likely shops for family gifts. That didn't take long, and I turned back towards the

Lunch by the Brule River.

lake, remembering, from the trip years earlier, a strip of
shore that jutted off from the town. Out by the sea wall,
I found the path and ambled along the lakeshore for
hours. I nestled under a bluff and watched the water lap
around my feet, and I discovered how easy it was to
experience a oneness with the scene. I walked farther
along the shore. The sky had remained bright, and the
sun sparkled on the water, flashing a million diamonds.
I sat alone on a small rise and became mesmerized,
remaining spellbound, losing all sense of time.
Contentment filled every fiber of my being, and a sense
of freedom severed the threads to physical concerns.

🐚 *Reflection:* Perfection is in this moment and in
every moment. I sit in pure consciousness that is
the allness of past, present, and future. There is
nothing else but consciousness, wherever I am,
whatever is my being. The power of life is in the
present moment. I vow to bring perfection forward, to be still in any situation and integrate this
realization. I think of a symbol I can use to remind
me "to let go and let the Universe prevail."

Before leaving town, I paid a visit to the Forest
Ranger station to inquire about the layout of Superior
National Forest. The Ranger steered me towards several

brochures that described the trails and roads. I asked about bears: "Would I meet any on the trails?" The Ranger's reply was comforting: "There are few bears seen on trails, rather one tends to see them more often around campsites and food parcels." If I saw one, his suggestion was to make a noise and better yet, to sing songs as I hiked. He said more harm came to hikers from elk during the rutting season, but since that was still a couple of months away, I was not to worry—"just hike and enjoy the forest," he said.

The next day I brought myself down to earth by doing laundry and chores in town. Afterwards, I found the golf course in a wooded area above town and played nine holes with two balls. It was a clear, sunny day, and temperatures were in the low sixties. Again, I was alone in my surroundings—it was like having a private golf course. My day ended with a glass of wine and meatloaf dinner; then, I curled up on the couch and read the brochures until late, highlighting the trails of interest.

Only twice during the month did I hear a noise or feel a presence near the cabin. I never investigated what kind of animal might be near; rather, I just trusted that my interior light would hold the visitors at bay.

The Fort at Grand Portage.

The Witch Tree.

The Witch Tree

BIG WAVES POUNDED the shore most of the night, introducing a gray new morning. Large, white-capped waves struck high upon the shoreline rocks; the wind and rain looked as if to remain throughout the day. I cozied up with a book most of the morning until shortly after noon when the clouds lifted and rays of sunshine beckoned me to take a hike.

I decided to head north towards the Canadian border and Grand Portage. It would be familiar ground, as I had made this jaunt during my previous visit to Grand Marais. Three things of interest were at Grand Portage. First there were the grounds and buildings of a fort where fur traders and Indians powwowed twice a year in the 1800s—once before the snows and again in the spring. Frenchmen and Indians portaged their furs out for trading with Englishmen of the fur company—the displays within the fort indicated one heck of a week-long party.

The second attraction was the steep walk up Rose Hill from where one could view the wide, deep glacier saddle and the portage trail out of Canada onto Lake Superior. I sat on a rock wall weaving stories about a trapper's solitary life until black clouds started to roll in and thunder sounded. I hurried back down the trail to my car in the parking lot.

Seven miles up the road was the third point of interest—the witch tree. Because of the storm I hesitated, yet my inner voice said "never mind the rain—go forward." Light sprinkles of rain fell on my windshield, but by the time I'd parked and walked towards the trail entrance, the rain had stopped. The path to the tree was narrow and winding and was covered with multicolored fall leaves. After a ten-minute walk, I came out onto a large rocky ledge with a commanding view over Lake Superior. A look to the right and one saw the witch tree.

This forest cedar grows out of the layered rocky bluff in only a smidgen of dirt collected in the corners of rock. Its roots wind down through the rocks, and its crown reaches at least twenty feet towards the sky. It has been a watchguard on that pinnacle for hundreds of years. The Chippewa Indians say four hundred years and call it a witch because it has grown without soil nourishment. For them, this is a sacred tree with special powers.

I sat in solitude with the tree, sun shining down on us. I was a witness to the marvels of growth and substance from invisible nourishment. On the distant shore was a rainbow, end to end over the water, with each stripe of color showing vibrantly. As I let the beauty melt into my being, a second rainbow spanned over the first, and then a third one. It was like finding a thousand lucky pennies. How could I not believe in the perfection of each moment as I gazed upon the three rainbows? It seemed like eons before they slowly faded and I heard voices coming through the woods.

These rainbows and their spell would recede into memory, but not the witchery of the tree. Just like an "open sesame," I sensed that a treasure was waiting to be seen.

Back in the car and halfway down the road, a vertical line of heavy rain snapped me back into present moment. To my amazement, the pavement was divided in two—one side totally dry and the other in a downpour. How unusual. Was this a symbol, a sign of some sort? I stopped the car—one half in rain, the other in dryness—and contemplated what it meant to cross its boundary line. The differences of one side from the other presented new experiences, feelings, and perceptions and therefore, new possibilities.

I was not ready to return to the cabin too quickly; I needed a slow transition. So, I decided to stop for high tea at the Naniboujou Lodge. I sat alone in the solarium, on a divan by the window, with a spectacular view of the lawn and lake. I watched a storm squall spread across the horizon. Old English tea and a plate of delicacies were quietly served as I reflected on the day. I thought of the freedom to be experienced and possibilities to be encountered if self-made boundaries and absolutes were relinquished. Letting go would require diligent efforts and new choices. My internal work was being laid out for me.

Third Insight: *What seems impossible can be possible. Your mind and limited knowledge can trick you into accepting boundaries that become self-limiting beliefs. Open up, begin to believe in possibilities, and they happen.*

Lake Agnes Trail

ON THE NINTH day, I drove into a remote area on the Gunflint road looking for hiking trails. The road curved through the thick forest, and I passed several lakes before I came upon a sign for the Northern Light Lake trail. The path was moderately steep and short; its beauty was at the crest where outstanding vistas spread in every direction and gave me a sense of the vastness of the Superior National Forest. I sat on a rock and let the stillness and awe envelop me. There is a thrill to being alone enclosed by nature, likened to the thrill of seeing unexpected beauty for the first time. Back on the road, I headed deeper onto Gunflint Trail, often driving under canopies of yellow leaves.

The yellow forest reached deeply into my psyche, as it seemed a true picture of the yellow forest frequently imaged in meditation. I had entered my imaginary yellow forest often to feel the quietness of strolling on the yellow leaf paths and to rest in a fancied hammock as I let go of unwanted negative aspects of my life. To find my yellow forest in real time, this day and many other days to come, seemed like an added blessing, and I sensed the release of boundaries.

I passed a sign noting that Lake Agnes was to the left and then searched for a trail entrance. Once again I was alone on a path, this one decorated with moss. I noticed how the soft, velvet moss clustered in different spots— on rocks, tree bark, fallen branches, and leaves. I saw its variegated hues of green and the small blue flowers born in its midst. It was all so delicate and lovely.

This path seemed to possess a deeper silence, and I could feel the life of the forest. Shortly, I began to feel apprehensive. It was a sense that something was nearby, unseen, and I wondered what I was to encounter. I wasn't prone to letting fear take over, but I did question whether I should proceed. A short banter of pros and cons ensued, from which I finally decided to expect the best and to continue on. Lake Agnes soon came into full view, presenting the ultimate in picturesque scenery— an absolute calm body of water like a mirror imprinting every tree along the bank. Since the trail paralleled the length of the lake, this scene was at my right for the entire walk. It seemed as if I was part of a painting on a large canvas.

Farther on, several sets of long-clawed paw prints showed fresh and well-defined in the soft mud of the path. I examined each set carefully, deciding the claws were too long and the paw too small for a bear. I also wondered if this animal was the presence I had sensed earlier on the path. Much later, with input from others, I surmised that maybe the tracks were those of wolverines—animals who are strong and aggressive.

It was late afternoon as I retraced the Gunflint Trail and drove into Grand Marais. I stopped for a cup of coffee on the porch of the bakery and watched the afternoon sun come to its close over Lake Superior. I sat in contemplation, knowing there was nothing else in this world but this moment and that I was opening up mentally to many possibilities. The vast, misty reaches of the Universe were at the horizon.

Bridge over the Onion River.

Leveaux Mountain

THE MIDDLE OF September was approaching, and the maples were deepening in color. Around midday on a Tuesday, I started out on the Leveaux Mountain path, entering through a grove of small trees and coming soon to a shallow but wide stream. As I stood on the bridge and savored the scene before me, I felt that I had come home. The peacefulness and nurturing spirit of this place seemed to bring back a remembrance, as if I had been here before.

The trail wound through woods, shaded by green glittering stands of birch, across a bridge over the Onion River, through little meadows, and up a hill under a rock overhang until I was at the crowns of the trees. The path looped around the mountain top and then came out to a large clearing. I followed the path around the edge, choosing the side with a view of the lake for my meditation. To my right was Sugar Loaf Mountain and its valleys of trees. I smiled at the lone red maple growing tall amid a stance of green fir trees—outstanding in all its beauty, unafraid to be unique. Beyond was an expanse of burgundy red maples and before me, flowing down to the lake, a patchwork of maple colors amid yellow aspens. And there I sat for a long time becoming at one with the moment.

Leveaux Mountain drew me back again before the end of the month. I often experienced a momentary twinge of anxiety when entering a trail—never so with Leveaux. There were no cars in the lot nor anyone on the trail the second time; afterwards, I knew that was best for what I had experienced.

I returned to the same rock and lookout upon reaching the top. As I sat silently in the sunshine, I had a sense of a presence behind me, although I had not heard any sound of a person approaching. I remained perfectly still and knew the presence was unworldly. My left shoulder seemed to feel the slight pressure of a hand, and I began a soundless communication, asking, "Who are you?"

"An Indian."

Again, I asked, "Who are you?"

"A wise old Indian."

I asked a third time, "Who are you?"

"A wise old soul who is going to be your guide."

"Why?" I replied.

"You are to receive wisdom and become a wise old soul yourself."

"In what way?" I inquired.

"I will walk with you until the wisdom is with you."

I waited until I felt alone again before rising from the rock. At the top of the trail, I stood overlooking the majestic forest. I was full of divine gratitude and wanted to honor its source; I sang "God Bless America" in my loudest voice, offering brotherly love note by note. By then, it was midafternoon, but I was not ready to go home. It had been a two-mile drive from the highway to the Leveaux entrance, and I decided to follow the road farther. It ended in a dead end amidst a large stand of yellow aspen. I walked for a while and then sat on a log in the golden forest; the silence of it was spine-tingling. And once again I felt a oneness with the moment and the yellow forest of meditation.

🐚 *Reflection:* What is it to be wise? Wisdom is of the Soul, the Spirit, and therefore, must be the essence of my Being. It has to be grounded in the very fundamental truths of the Universe, truths known down through the ages. To be wise, one must understand the truth and manifest its rightness in thought and action. I vowed to listen with all my senses and to be an attentive learner.

I stopped by Lutsen Lodge on the way home for a slice of their famous blueberry pie and a cup of coffee in their dining room overlooking Lake Superior. It seemed the wise thing to do.

Cascade Falls

THIS DAY WAS Tom's birthday—memories of the love of my life flooded into my consciousness upon awakening. There were no barriers to rethinking the highs and lows of the eight-year love affair, a relationship which had ended ten years ago. The perplexities of love seem to be varied and require fine definition. I realized how unwise I'd been about the aspects of love and knew when I had dishonored love in my life. Since beginning my spiritual journey, I'd studied different interpretations of love other than just the love born out of desire. I wanted to ponder this subject further and knew I might find inspiration beside water.

Down the highway from Leveaux was Cascade Park, with fifteen miles of trails intersecting with a fast flowing stream—exactly as described in the ranger's brochure. I hiked the afternoon, following a path that wound gradually upward past four waterfalls. The forest was very quiet, and the rush of falling water offered a cleansing effect that I embraced with all my senses. My mind likened the flow of life to the flow of water: ever moving in one direction, rolling over or around obstacles, changing between shallowness and depth, sometimes muddy, sometimes crystal clear. My body felt rejuvenated and coupled with the surroundings.

I continued on up the trail. What appeared to be a chicken standing on the path above me was a grouse. It flew onto a nearby log and posed for a picture. Soon after I saw pad prints with large claws at my feet similar to the ones seen at Lake Agnes. Wolverines or bears? As I crossed a grassy clearing, a startled deer bounded away, its outline facing me in the dense bushes as I passed.

Walking through the quietness of a forest brings a never-ending sense of purity and peace. I knew these experiences in the north woods would be implanted in my consciousness, to be easily recalled and serve as inspiration for the rest of my life. Around a bend, I came upon a small area of downed trees on a bluff overlooking a ravine in the forest beyond. The opening was like a natural living room with a large window, a perfect seat for meditation.

🐚 *Reflection:* The song "Looking for Love in All the Wrong Places" marched across my mind. Looking for love to come to me from the persons of my affection in order to fill my personal desires had been my pattern. It had not worked. Love is not a payoff for something done or sacrifice made. Like happiness, love is a state of mind that builds from one's choices and thinking. Might love be the sustaining power of the spirit? And if it is, I must love unconditionally, without judgment, minus expectations. First within, then without. First Ann, begin by closing down the judgments and giving of yourself without expectations of return. Let go of the old ways and embrace the new.

My thoughts, as I walked out of Cascade Falls, centered on the many daily opportunities I had for learning how to give of self without expecting payoffs. Simple acts came to mind, like listen more than talk, let others speak first with their stories, and give because I want to give versus wanting reciprocation. My motivation was strong as I headed back to the cabin. It was early to bed and early to rise.

The greeting of dawn displayed a variety of hues as the sun rose behind a soft layer of clouds. The new morning began with a strong sense of well-being and resolution.

Fourth Insight: *The strength of our Being is far greater than one understands or appreciates. If one keeps the four aspects of Being—physical, social, spiritual, mental—in balance, life can be a divine experience. Choosing the degree of balance is an individual responsibility and at one's option.*

Oberg

IT WAS SUNDAY, and I was eager to be in the forest after extremely heavy rainfall had kept me confined to the cabin for two days. Although the forest would be wet, more Sunday hikers would be on the trails due to the promise of a sixty-two-degree temperature and maples in full color. People in Minnesota await fall days such as these, and Oberg Mountain, across from Leveaux, is a favorite choice, for it is heavily populated with aspens and maples.

The trail did not ascend to the mountain peak; rather, it circled around the mountain and offered many lookouts. No doubt because of the magnificent beauty before the eyes, each viewpoint was like a porch with benches inviting one to stay. And people were doing just that, crowded together in silence. I turned towards a

greeting of "Hi, Ann" and discovered a coworker standing by my side. He and his friends were interested in my
reason for being there, and they oohed and aahed as I
described the cabin and my days.

I found myself in the midst of more people than I
preferred and decided to return again to Oberg during

Perch in tree where I sat in contemplation.

a weekday. The second time around, the trees were more yellow, and I was walking through the golden forest again. As I passed the entrance post, a chipmunk sat on a log next to the trail. The poor little creature was crazed with something in his ears and was digging so intently he was oblivious to everything. Even when I spoke, he didn't move. I walked on, wondering how much I'd not heard due to negligent listening habits.

The trail wound around the outside of the bluff for a while and then turned back into the golden forest. On one of the inner paths, I came upon a brilliant cluster of trees that halted me in my tracks. I stood spellbound, reluctant to proceed. I wanted to touch and hold someone. So I put my arms around a tree, my cheek against its bark, and closed my eyes.

A voice spoke: "Are you taking spirit from the tree, or is it giving spirit to you?" As I replied "Both," I turned around and came face-to-face with a pair of clear blue eyes. He was slight in stature, a finely-lined face topped with a denim beret.

He shared these words: "Isn't it strange that people do not hear the music of nature. I've seen people walking through woods with earplugs, listening to taped music when the most beautiful music of all surrounds them. We stand in the midst of a symphony, but one must listen to hear the notes. Hug many trees and listen, they have messages for us." He then quoted a poem by Longfellow about how the wind in the forest was God playing a symphony.

I thanked him as he started up the long path to the turn in the trail. I noticed that he walked slowly with a limp, as if one leg was shorter than the other. My eyes dropped for just a moment, and I decided I wanted to walk with him. When I looked up, there was no one on the trail. It was not possible that the man could have reached the curve of the path in a single moment. I stood in bewilderment. A few feet off the path, I spied a perch in the limbs of a tree, and climbing up, I sat mystified by what I had just experienced.

The rest of my walk was full of reflections on the purpose, as I understood it, for this retreat. Silence, stillness, enlightenment, and learn to listen were the words the inner voice had uttered. I now realized at the deepest level of my being that I must change my ways. My efforts must concentrate on removing the clutter from my consciousness and my physical space. Listen more intently and actively seek to understand. Make room for possibilities to manifest themselves and be watchful of self-imposed boundaries. And, continue to follow and trust the intuitive voice.

My car stood alone in the parking lot as I came off the trail. An unearthly aura surrounded and permeated me. I was reluctant to leave the woods, so I drove up to the now familiar aspen grove at the end of Onion River Road and sat in the yellow forest. It was a perfect place for reverie and to let the messages of the day sink into my consciousness. I headed off for home around five o'clock and put my mind that evening to writing.

Fifth Insight: *One must have open channels to hear messages of the Universe. To understand a message, one must be an in-the-moment listener, clear of binding emotions, judgments or preconceived labels. Knowledge and wisdom wait to enter and can only do so when mental earplugs are removed.*

Writing

MANY OF MY coworkers urged me, over several years, to become a writer. I couldn't see this capability as strongly as they and lent no credence to their suggestions—until this retreat. I had packed a book given to me by Rebecca, one of my strong supporters, and toward the end of the second week, I gave the book undivided attention for several nights.

Writing the Natural Way (by Gabriele Lusser Rico) presented theory, techniques, and exercises for creating different forms of writing. I was fascinated with my compositions and the ease in which words flowed onto paper. I was hooked and became engrossed each night; three or four hours would pass without notice, and often midnight came as a surprise.

When I left the cabin retreat, I also left the discipline

of doing writing exercises. Thirteen years later, I read the pieces written in 1988 and felt encouraged to begin again. I'd like to think that I am preparing to become a distinguished writer in my next incarnation.

One of the 1988 pieces resonates particularly with the retreat.

My Cabin

IT WAS A gift received with joy, a miracle producing more than expected, magic performing a disappearing act. Gone were the demands, gone were the bindings, gone were the obligations. Here was the solitude that quieted the mind, the isolation that soothed the nerves, the laziness that healed the body. It was the haven protected in the forest—my haven, my retreat, my cabin, my September gift.

Your time has come to sing a song
    heard in the symphony played in the trees
    orchestrated with the instruments of
    maple, ash, birch, and evergreens.
Your time has come to sing a song
    heard in the sounds of the kettle-drum waves
    played by the musician whose beat is the
    force of Eternity.

Your time has come to sing your song
 heard in the musical words of the birds
 written in notes and scales by
 jays, sparrows, warblers, and chickadees.
Your time has come to sing your song
 heard under the baton of the Master Conductor
 the melody strong, sung full-voiced for all
 to hear of the lyrics learned.
Your time has come to sing your song.

To The Rescue

A STEADY, HEAVY rainfall kept me cabin-bound for a day, and I was eager to get into the woods, which would be crisp, bright, and refreshed by rain. The sky held the type of clouds that typically gave way to sunshine. It was now the third week of September, and temperatures had dropped from the sixties to mid-fifties. I decided to drive south past the Leveaux/Oberg turn off and onto the Sawbill Hill road. This would take me to two twin peaks facing each other across meadows.

I walked Britton Peak first, the highest trail on the North Shore at 927 feet. The steep trail followed lovely, high, grassy meadows showing signs that here were favorite sleeping beds for deer. It was a gorgeous day, with sun sparkling through yellow trees and white puffs of clouds moving overhead.

Another panorama where "Wow" is the only response. At the top of the peak were the hard rocks left when melting glaciers washed away all the soft elements. The bright colors of the trees were turning to the dullness of deeper color variations. I pushed away the thought that my days remaining could be counted in single digits.

Carleton Peak was a twin of Britton, and it showed as such when looking from peak to peak. There was no bottom trail connecting the two peaks; each had separate entry points from separate parking lots. Enjoying the views from the top of Carleton Peak, I watched through binoculars as two hawks were joined by two, three, and then five more—all searching for midday meals. Their ease and swirls of flight brought back an old memory of gliding I had done in Arizona. The quietness of riding air currents matched the quietness before me.

Midafternoon was approaching, and I decided to return to town for coffee and a treat on the bakery porch. I also wanted some cards for notes to family and friends. As I headed the car back to the highway, the following inner conversation took place. The voice said, "Let's go up the Onion River road to the aspen grove." ("No," I thought, "the color wouldn't have changed much since my last visit there.")

The voice said, "Go." ("Yeah, and if I do, I'll be late into town.")

The voice replied, "Go, you won't get cards to-day anyway." ("Well, I'd like to have them to do my writing.")

The voice came back with, "Go up the road—you can get your cards tomorrow. Just go, you'll enjoy the scenery." ("O.K., O.K., I hear you.")

I followed the directive and took the turnoff to the aspen grove. About three quarters of the way I passed a van with doors open; I noted two women and a child. When I reached the end of the road, I didn't stay long, as the voice said, "Let's go." ("Good. I can get my cards.")

"No, no cards today—just go back down the road." I knew then that the women needed help, so I returned immediately to the van, finding them anxious and concerned.

The younger woman, Pat, introduced me to her mother, who was holding the hands of a small girl about three years old. Pat was nursing a baby and told me that her husband had headed into the woods on a mainte-nance road over two hours ago. He had taken his gun to hunt for grouse and said he would return in thirty min-utes. Pat described her husband as an expert woodsman, so his tardiness was worrisome to her. Because it was a spur-of-the-moment idea, he did not have all of the usual hiking gear with him, such as compass, matches, or warm jacket. She did not want to drive from the area for help, in case he came out of the woods.

I asked them how I could help, and we developed a plan of action. Pat and I would take the child and drive to the ranger's station by Tofte to get rescue help before they closed. Luckily, I'd noticed the station earlier in the day and could drive there quickly. Her mother and the baby would stay behind with the van. When Pat and I returned, I would take the mother and the little girl back to the condos where they were vacationing for a couple of days. When this was all done, I would stay with Pat and the baby until Dwight, her husband, had been found.

We arrived at the ranger station ten minutes before their closing. The ranger informed us that the sheriff's office was the rescue unit, and she offered to make the call. Pat told them the circumstances and received the reply, "Someone will be on the way as soon as possible." We went back to the van and proceeded with our plan. The sheriff arrived just as I returned from the condo to wait with Pat.

The sheriff said he would drive the length of the maintenance road using the car horn and loudspeaker to draw a response from Dwight. If that failed, he would need to get other helpers to work a nighttime rescue. As Pat and I walked with the baby we could hear the noise of the loudspeaker and car horn go from loud to soft as the sheriff rode farther into the forest. Darkness was approaching, and I could sense Pat's apprehension. I spoke encouraging words, although I had a premonition that Dwight might have turned an ankle and could not walk. Just as darkness descended, the rescue vehicle drove out of the woods—with Dwight.

Dwight had violated Hiker's Rule #1 by straying from a marked trail and had lost his bearings. Thinking he knew the direction to go, he walked into the soft mire of a beaver dam where a shoe was sucked off. With his ankle twisted, no shoe, and receiving no response to several gunshots, he decided he was in trouble. He was down to his last bullet, which he knew had to be saved. He then followed Hiker's Rule #2 by staying in one spot to await rescue and began pulling leaves and under-growth together to keep warm when the sun went down. The sheriff was ready to go for more help when he heard Dwight's faint response, and finally the search was over. As I left, Dwight was still shaking his head over how an experienced hiker could have left a marked trail without a compass.

For me, Rule #1: Never ignore the intuitive voice; it's my compass. No one else had traveled that particular section of the road but me—seems I had been sent to Pat and her family to be their Good Samaritan.

The moon was full when I walked out on the deck at ten o'clock that evening. I put on a jacket and went down to sit by the lake. Misty clouds had melted away, and the moon, whole and white, turned the lake into a silver sheen. Mars sat east of the moon, with its reddish glow, jiggling in the sky. It all seemed real and unreal at the same time. Later in bed, I felt blessed to have the moon shining on my pillow as I went to sleep.

Temperance River

THE DAY OPENED with bright sunshine swimming across the lake and a promise of sixty-degree weather, a great incentive for an early start. I decided to drive farther back along Gunflint Trail, where I found the dirt road either canopied with trees or open to far-reaching lush meadows or paralleling pristine lakes. I drove seventy miles and stopped often just to gaze or to take pictures. I walked Caribou Trail, which was as beautiful as others I'd taken, and stopped by lakes just to laze in the sunshine.

Back in town, I lunched on the bakery porch and read the history of Temperance River, where I had decided to spend the afternoon. The river starts shallow and widens higher up the trail, then swirls forcefully through deep narrow gorges for nearly a mile and finally opens to a wide bay before flowing into Lake Superior. The Temperance River is the choice of fishermen; on this day they were scattered all over the bay.

As I studied the formation and depth of the gorges, I thought of the time it took the cutting power of water to design the inner walls of the gorges. They looked as if they had been sculptured by an artist.

Reflection: I made an analogy to my own life, wondering what designs I had cut on inner walls of self and others. Spoken words, inner thoughts, actions, and facial expressions flow through every moment of a day, carving impressions often not to be erased. Be still and listen before words or action. Be kind in the use of them. Be sincere with praise and encouragement. All admirable traits to be practiced.

I walked alongside the water either by its edge or higher up on cliffs, and the narrow stream finally grew to a wide river. The Temperance is full of boulders of all sizes, and its water is pure and clear to the bottom of the riverbed. My eyes spied a huge flat-top boulder up ahead perfectly placed in the middle of the river. As I came near, I saw that there were enough smaller stepping rocks for me to reach the boulder without getting too wet.

Mouth of Temperance River, a favorite fishing spot for fishermen.

Boulder in midstream where I lounged peacefully.

There I lounged peacefully, and, like honey sliding down a stick, relaxation slid through my body. The music of John Denver sang through my mind: "You fill up my senses, come fill me again . . . come let me love you, let me love you again" or "There are many ways of being in a circle we call life . . . you are never alone, spirit fills the darkness . . ."

A great sense of peace enveloped me, and tears of pure joy wet my cheeks. I became one with that moment, a sensation of oneness with the pine trees of the forest, the rock and stones, the water and ripples, the blue sky and sun. I left the sensation of space for the voice of the universe. The breeze caressed my soul, seeming to say, "I love you, I love you, I love you." I'd reached the core of being; I was in the realm of divine experience.

There was no hurry to leave. I bathed my feet in the cold water. I sang a love song. I gave thanks to the Creator of all things. I forgave my prior ignorance. I relished the gifts given to me this month. I promised to adopt a new way of living.

I went farther up the trail, which extended for miles all the way to Duluth. My inclination was to walk on and on, but I did so for only thirty minutes. With reluctance, I reversed my direction and headed back, bringing with me a profound sense of spirituality. This day never ended.

Moose Mountain

ONE LAST LONG hike into the forest took me into the mountains, into the meadows, a remote area away from the lake and rivers. The trails on Moose Mountain were varied—some well-trodden and some only a single-file track in the grass. The forest was absolute stillness in the lower meadows, and the outer world was far removed from me. Like a forest animal, I felt at home and wanted to walk every trail. After a steep climb to the top of a ridge, I found a circle of grass where I ate lunch and then lay back, musing on the surroundings.

🍃 *Reflection:* Our spiritual growth comes through Christ consciousness. Spiritual growth is like seeds in the forest, pushing themselves up through spiritual soil, growing into beings of Christ consciousness. The seed that holds the secrets, the unknown, the essence of life, vanishes and leaves in its place a tall spiritual being. Forests of them. A Christ forest, each an individual consciousness growing in its own way and arriving at a universal oneness, a collective consciousness.

Farther along the path, I stopped on a ridge where a canyon extended down and across to another ridge of trees. My mind dwelt on how a tree grew from a single seed, and I likened it to my beginning from a single seed. That a tiny seed held all the elements of growth was a mystery of the universe. I fancied myself a tree and envisioned the seed bursting open with sprouts. As the seed disappeared, the sprouts gave growth to a lovely tree. I felt at one with the silent forest; slowly a gentle rustling breeze entered that solemn silence.

I found a new peace on Moose Mountain, one that remained with me from that day forward. I left fear behind and understood the beauty of acceptance—a belief in a higher order. I knew that this experience would be reaffirmed every time I felt and heard the rustling of a breeze.

Sixth Insight: *Everything works in perfect order, the intent of the Universe. Perfect order was yesterday, is today, and will be* *tomorrow. One would not know pleasure if one did not know pain. One would not know happiness if one did not know sorrow. One would not know success if one did not know failure. One would not know if one did not listen. Like a coin, every happening in life has two sides, and one must experience both sides of the coin to know perfect order.*

Last visit to Witch Tree.

A Day of Farewells

MY PLAN FOR the day was to revisit Kettle Falls and the witch tree and then follow any other fancy as it occurred. I fortified myself with a hearty meal at Naniboujou Lodge, choosing the Logger's Breakfast—strong coffee, meat, potatoes, eggs, homemade bread, and milk. From there I made my way back to Kettle Falls to retrace a bit of my first hike.

The varied shades of trees were now gone; just the green firs colored the canyon. The water was the same copper color and running a bit higher. I walked as far as the middle falls and stood on the first overlook point and thought of myself as I had first viewed this scene—the freshness of my eyes, the eagerness of my spirit, the openness to my thoughts. The past month came together as just a single experience, and I knew a considerable transformation had taken place. The first day at Kettle Falls had been a beginning, and this last day was also a beginning. I gave blessings to the water spirits.

There was a mile-and-a-half service road leading from the parking lot, and I walked it up to a campsite. I let the quiet stillness seep into every part of my body; I chanted, I hugged trees, I sang "God Bless America" and watched a large flock of Canada geese fly overhead. I heard distinctly the swishing of their wings and smiled at their perfect order. Just as I did, one goose came forward from the left side of the V and replaced the leader. I gave blessings to the animal spirits.

My next stop was at the witch tree. I painted a sky from memories of rainbows. I put my hands on the tree, contemplating the flow of life through its exposed roots and the longevity that had resulted. What a marvel to witness the nourishment provided by the universe for all things. The presence of the ancient Indian, now an accepted guide of my spirit, stood with me, and I welcomed the companionship as I gave blessings to the earth and sky and then left reluctantly.

I drove back through town, turning on the road going up to Maple Hill Cemetery. Years before, my friend had brought me to this cemetery with her belief that this was the most beautiful cemetery of all. It sat on top of a hill with a small chapel in the midst of maple trees. I particularly remembered a large tree by the chapel. Like Siamese twins, it had two separate trees growing from a single trunk about five feet up from the soil. What a disappointment when I found only the left-side tree remaining—it made for distortion and a blemish upon this lovely spot and upon my memory. Yet it was a reminder that change is a principle of life; one must let go of attachments, both physical and mental, to ease into the cycle of change . . . "one must experience both sides of the coin to know the full experience."

I walked the grounds and finally chose a tombstone to sit beside in the sunshine. It was time to bury some old habits and leave them behind.

The first thing to bury must be *controlling behavior.* How could I now believe that only I knew what was best and how to do it? I saw in attempting to control situations, I deflected a purer timing for outcomes and end results. I realized, also, that awareness of present moments is lost in the controlling actions.

The next thing to bury was *judgmental thinking.* How could I really ever know the inner makeup of any human being? I saw in judging others, I denied them the acknowledgment that they were doing the best they could with what they had. I realized, also, that kindness and freedom are negated with judgmental thoughts.

One last thing to bury was the *need for recognition.* Why must I compete and drive for affirmations that I am O.K.? I saw in feeding my egocentric needs, I had instilled a falseness in my motivation. I realized, also, that trust and integrity are diluted by this self-need.

I knew that I'd have to exercise new practices if I were to leave these old ways behind. My higher self quickly proposed the virtues to integrate into my being. They were all very logical and consistent with the experiences of this retreat, and I accepted the ideas and committed myself to a different course of behavior. A new intention was born.

    Reflection: Become love and kindness. Be generous with time, thoughts, encouragement, and listening. Seek to see the reality of each situation encountered and the wholeness of the interacting persons. Portray universal love—study and master its attributes. Honor personal dignity. Trust the Universe and its processes.

    Reflection: Be still and listen. Maintain awareness in present moment. Seek clarity and balance in each situation. Remain open to all concepts and possibilities. Remember that each experience has two sides—know them both. Trust the Higher Self and honor the intuitive voice. Choose what is right to do and give full measure to it with purity of heart.

I knew what I had to do and knew I must begin now. The changes were big, and it would take patience, tolerance, and lots of awareness to integrate the new virtues and to witness their manifestation in my daily life. I would set no deadlines. I would allow progress to occur, and I would nurture a new mindfulness. In the largest scheme of things the journey itself, not the destination, was the most important. On this thought, I gave blessings to the human spirit.

It was late afternoon and almost nine hours since breakfast. I drove back with a deep sense of satisfaction and a crisp, clear perspective of the universe. I saw the paradox: I was nothing, yet I was everything. I was not needed in the greater realms of the universe, but I could make a difference.

That difference had to have the highest value I could put to it. I was now ready to make corrections to the course of my journey.

That evening I bundled myself in warm wraps and

sat on the rocky point below the cabin. The wind was
cold and waves were heavy, gaining momentum before
the storm that arrived the following day. I meditated on
how the lake had influenced me.

> The heavy, crashing waves had battered through
>   the mundane
> They'd washed away old residue
> They'd pulled me towards oneness
> They'd liquefied the past
> They'd made powerful the present
> The gentle, lapping waves had soothed the fears
> They'd fed my Spirit
> They'd flowed into the Divine
> They'd made easy my own transformation

Good-Bye

I HAD BEEN gathering my belongings all week, and my last tasks were doing laundry and cleaning appliances. I went into the laundromat first and then came back to the kitchen. It was a cold, wet morning after a night of heavy rains; the clouds still were dripping showers off and on. In early afternoon, my chores complete, I headed up towards the highway to take the three-mile walk around Croftsville. This inner road was close to the lake, giving me an opportunity to enjoy the water one more time. I purposely dismissed any thought of tomorrow or my leaving.

The grassy point by the greenhouse beckoned me for one more pensive moment; I had sat here so often during the month. To the south was a triangular band of whiteness framed by an otherwise gray sky. I studied that white streak of light.

🕓 *Reflection:* I can only see what I am capable of seeing at any point in time, and just because I have not seen the reality behind the veil does not mean that reality is not present. God is reality and is the source of life, love, and being—the substance, the essence of who I am. That source is eternal—here forever and ever. See beyond the veil, Ann, see beyond the cloud, see beyond the gray matter, see through to the Light. Be the Light.

It was a peaceful evening of reading, sitting on the porch, walking down the path to the lake. And then I slept into my last morning. As I placed the first items in the car, I broke down in racking sobs. The tears would not stop, and at times I could hardly see. The pain of disengagement doubled me up, and I sat down on the porch steps. This retreat had been a once-in-a-lifetime experience during which a personal transformation had taken place—the most meaningful in my life. Some of my tears were of joy and gratitude for even having had the experience. Some were of sorrow—like leaving a part of me behind, even though I knew that this experience had been etched forever inside of me. Some tears fell because I was unready to return to the mundane life. I often wondered how many days I could have stayed in solitude. Maybe, after a certain time, there would have been no coming back.

I finally got myself composed enough to drive away, and I did not look back until I was at that bend in the road where I had first viewed Grand Marais. I stood there again for few moments recalling those earlier impressions and saying my actual good-bye. With a heavy heart, but also one full of gratitude, I began my reentry.

Outside Two Harbors is Baptism Falls, and I could not resist the temptation to take one more hike. The falls is a favorite trail of a friend, who'd highly recommended it. I took the path to the lower falls, thinking then I would decide if I had time to go farther, as I wanted to be back in the city before darkness.

Footsteps on the forest floor were silenced by inches of wet, wet leaves, so I moved along quickly without a sound. I was happy to be back in the forest and matched my stillness to the silence of the trail. What a surprise when I saw a black bear enter from the brush onto the path, luckily heading away from me. The bear, about waist high, was in no hurry, so I surmised that he was unaware of me. I might have been just part of the forest. I watched without fear and held still while the bear lumbered up the path, finally disappearing back into brush. Should I continue or forego seeing the falls? I went on another twenty minutes to the falls, where I talked with two other hikers. They'd seen scat but no bear. I was grateful that the first bear to appear had been on my last walk in the forest. Bears are symbols of good fortune to some, and under that definition, I treasured the experience.

It was a beautiful drive into Duluth and then into Minneapolis. The trees were in full color, and I was to enjoy an extended fall season. The colorful trees would reaffirm the Lake Superior retreat—the learning experiences, the new insights, and my resolve towards commitments made. I returned with an expanded consciousness and a brighter journey to travel. And, I now knew what perfect order could be.

Seventh Insight: Light is a wonderful symbol for Christ Consciousness. Just because that light gets covered by the gray veil of humanity does not negate the principle of God—the I Am that I Am. Just because one cannot see the sun behind the gray clouds does not mean the sun is not there. Human perception can be a veil; human concepts can be limited; human behavior can cover the light.

Last three-mile walk around Croftsville.

Epilogue

THE 1988 RETREAT was a parenthesis in time and reached me at the deepest of levels. I was fifty-eight years of age at the time and know that any maturity I had attained by that age brought broader aspects to the retreat and my understanding of its experience. In the intervening years, I have watched the stream of learnings received by the water and under the trees gain strength and become a part of my daily life. Old ways fade slowly, weaving in and out of behavior; but evidence, over time, shows they do fade.

I can now love without holding expectations. I no longer give in order to receive nor seek love from the face of another. Love comes from inside, gives in quietness, and desires nothing in return.

I can live in stillness and enjoy long times in solitude. I still work on present moment awareness and to be there without an agenda. In quiet states, I learn much by listening to my surroundings and welcoming broader perspectives.

I feel awakened to the Divinity of life, which I believe must be the mantle before birth. It is no longer necessary for me to be right. I can let go and let things be revealed. It is a marvel at how the Universe processes in perfect order, even more freely when the ego stays out of the way.

I returned to Moose Mountain one fall day for a friend's wedding. I elected to stay the full weekend to walk the trails of Leveaux and Oberg Mountains. They were picture perfect to the memory held in my mind during the years past. I tap into 1988 easily at any time, anywhere, and have relived those thirty days a hundred times over. I read my journal frequently and melt into happiness when viewing my tray of slides.

I listen attentively to my inner voice, and I wonder how long I would have waited for my transformation if I had ignored those messages of the early eighties. It showed me the excellence by which the Universe orchestrates events. I hold faith in its processes every day.

And about the "ancient Indian." His guidance was with me for six years as he helped me to see things in a broad wholeness rather than in myopic pieces. He taught me the wisdom of patience and thinking broadly before taking action. He brought me up short when I looked with limiting or self-serving thoughts. His guidance was full of keys for my learning. His presence departed one afternoon during a meditation, leaving me a more enlightened traveler on my spiritual journey. I learned that doing the right thing, in the right way, at the right time, with the right intention was the essence of his teaching. And so, this is my wisdom.

ABOUT THE AUTHOR

Ann Wade enjoyed a varied business career spanning thirty-six years in marketing, sales, general management, resource development, training and motivational speaking. In 1996, she realized her dream of being a consultant for small businesses.

Wade spent thirty days in solitude in 1988, which changed her life immensely and inspired the writing of this book. She retired to Iowa City in 2001 and now fulfills another dream of being a writer.